Phoenix: poems

Copyright © 2022 by Deveree Extein

First Edition - 2022

Book design by Deveree Extein
Edited by Shelby Leigh
Illustrations by Canva

ISBN
978-1-0879-2071-9

deveree extein

phoenix

deveree extein

phoenix

For the ones who burn and burn

deveree extein

PHOENIX

poems by
Deveree Extein

deveree extein

INTRODUCTION

<u>phoe·nix</u>
<u>/ˈfēniks/</u>
noun

(in classical mythology) a unique bird that lived for five or six centuries in the Arabian desert, after this time burning itself on a funeral pyre and rising from the ashes with renewed youth to live through another cycle.
- Oxford Dictionary

I have waited so long to set these words down and weave them together to illustrate the story of the phoenix. From the burning to the rising, this poetry collection is a testament that I have survived everything that has tried to extinguish me. I invite you on my journey of healing. To take a peek inside my world of flames and see if you can withstand the heat.

Phoenix has been a dream of mine for so many years. It all started with *Flicker*, the initial spark that soon enveloped everything I knew in fire. I burned down and tore through the ashes to rise anew. Now it continues with *Phoenix*.

Watch how I take flight.

deveree extein

Author's Note

Phoenix should be handled with care. There are
poems that may be triggering; covering topics such
as mental illness, anxiety, suicidal ideation, grief,
body image, and sexual assault.
Take care of yourself.

deveree extein

phoenix

NICE TO MEET YOU, I'M DEVEREE

I've always dreamed
of spitting out shards of my teeth
but I still don't know what it means
never thought I'd live past eighteen
but can we keep that between you and me?
sometimes I feel a little crazy
so I distract myself daily
I don't want to deal with these memories
reminiscing might be the death of me
or maybe crippling insecurity
only everything worries me

WRITER'S BLOCK PART I

Every time this pen touches the paper
I must resist the violent urge to
immortalize my heartbreak
to dress it up in its Sunday best
and show it off as a golden trophy

I must strip it down to its rawest form
to moon-white bone, skeleton
with no pretty skin to hide behind

to see how truly ugly it is
this savage beast, raging monster
that climbs through my mouth
to scream its woes into the world

I haven't touched the pen in some time
to hold the creature at bay
it is voiceless
but still ever so present

A BATTLE WITH MY BRAIN

My mind is a war zone
where the only casualty
is me

THE BLUES

Depression greets me warmly
in the morning
like a dog with a bird
tight in its mouth
paws at the gray of
my front door
waiting for my eyes
to flutter open
and these tired hands to stretch

Soon
the slow crackling of consciousness
creeps across
this rotting brain
electrifying every neuron
shocking me fully awake

and then it isn't quiet anymore

Full volume
static leaking from my ears
a hand hovers over the dial
but cannot choose a station
it's all **loud loud loud**
the pounding of drums and
the shrill scream of a guitar
smooth saxophone
and vibrant pulsing techno beats

phoenix

a heartbeat
and the clattering of piano keys
two hands just slamming *down down down*
the cacophony settles
between my eyes
nestling deeper into the quietest folds of my mind
until there is no other
sound heard
but
the blues

THE RAGDOLL PART I

Is made up of pieces of
everyone she has ever met
she created herself in the image
of everyone she has ever loved
parts of every heart
she has ever touched
thump loudly in her chest

Ophelia

Cool blue
deep pool
you didn't
know what
I was going
through

serene dream
beautiful scene
climbing into
a willow tree

now out of sight
goodnight
goodnight

disappearance
cold dark kiss
weightlessness
pure bliss

TW: SEXUAL ASSAULT

PAPER GIRL

His scissor hands slid down my skin
Split me at the seams
I came undone in the worst way
My once tightly sewn stitches
Ripped open
Everything I was made of laid at our feet

The vision of him taking it all for himself
is burned into my eyelids
if they ever close again
I would relive those moments

I'm watching water circle the drain
before finally slipping into the pipes
and away from me
forever
as I'm spitting shiny shards of teeth
into my trembling hands
and wiping furiously
at the corners of my mouth
where the blood is drying, crusting over

my knees are an unnamable shade of blue
maybe it's violet
or black
something reminiscent
of a midnight sky

phoenix

I sit in this porcelain casket
scrubbing away the disgusting traces of him
and mourn
my innocence
and birth my rage

the water begins to run clear
but I can still see
nasty festering open wounds
I slide off the mangled, tortured body
and step into one
that is a little too big for me

I bury thirteen-year-old me
and hope to forget the memory
of this tragedy

LIAR

Maybe when the blood stops flowing from my mouth / I can spit out the name of the culprit / but through splintered teeth and busted lip / I manage to utter an apology / I've buried the hatchet under my tongue / and stitched up my Chelsea smile / hung the bleached linens out to dry / and simmered in the summer breeze / it burned just like his touch / They ask me, *Well, who did this?* / I say, *A man.* / A burning man / with hard eyes and rough hands / a man / whose life will go on unscathed / unaffected by the violence / he pours into the world / when you find me naked and wrapped in cellophane / tied up like a bow on your child's Christmas gift / you will ask *What happened?* / But you will not believe me / label me **liar** / instead of *victim* / he kisses his children good morning / and I suckle the blood from my wounds / the white flag is red now / I do not know the taste of forgiveness anymore / the blade splits my tongue / and forces the stitches to pop / I scream

phoenix

TW: Sexual Assualt

When (otherwise) peaceful women go berserk, what ticks them off

Your vile tongue / dripping with venom / you see me / make my way / around the street corner / and you fly off your hidden perch / following me closely / I can feel / your hot breath / on my neck / I can hear / you begging / for a chance / to taste the salt / on my skin / the "You look gorgeous, mama!" / "You got a boyfriend?" / "Give me that pussy, girl" / the catcalls / crawl under my epidermis / like a parasite / nestling deep under muscle / you're closer now / close enough to touch / "Where you going, beautiful?" / "I could make you feel real good, you know" / "Turn around, bitch!" / and I do / in the face of danger / I morph into a monster / to match the one standing before me / and I show all of my teeth / extend my claws / and I tear you apart /

HEAVY

I wish I could
blow my memories
and silly little feelings
to smithereens
they're too heavy
to carry

HEADSPACE

My mind isn't a very nice place to be sometimes
a rotting, stinking city
a festering, open wound
dank, damp, and dark
a melodic hum rattles the flickering streetlights
thick claws of fog creep through the alleyways
there is a sense of urgency
of restlessness
everything is still but my mind is racing
everything is quiet but my mind is loud
it is folding and unfolding on itself
eating itself, like some kind of sick snake
I cut my skull to release the pressure
blood doesn't scare me anymore
it doesn't run red here

SHOWER TIME

Quietly setting this bag of bones
onto the shower floor
I lose my mind
this white room becomes my safe haven
when the wooden door locks
and the water runs
tears pour from my eyes
the uncontrollable, sheer force
of emotion explodes in my chest
and brain
but is concealed by wet hands
over aching mouth
then
it all ends
the outburst washes away
spinning down into the
drain

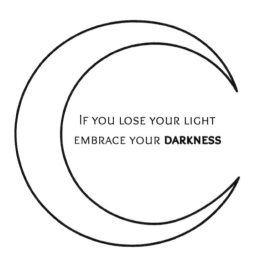

If you lose your light
embrace your **DARKNESS**

TRINKETS

I rummage through
the drawers of my mind
tossing every little hidden trinket
that was left behind
so I will not be haunted by
your memory

SYMPHONY 2.0

Sometimes when I listen to a song
it is not the musician's voice I hear
but yours
in the sweet murmurs of longing
and in the raspy rhymes of regret
your soft twang echoes
behind layers of production
whispering "baby"
between the banging of a heavy drum

I'm always finding our names / in the melodies / like I'm
the one / who wrote the song

FORBIDDEN FRUIT

We sit under the high afternoon sun
I watch you peel an orange
quickly yet delicately
just like you undress me
you offer me the first piece
I part my lips
for you to place it on my tongue
but you reach past my teeth
down my throat and
bust through my rib cage
before grabbing a chunk of my heart
you yank it out
my eyes trace the trails of
blood and spit and nectar
running down the tattoo on your arm
you flash me a toothy grin
and take a bite

Infinite playlist

Even in sin-stained sheets
you lie your head
next to mine and whisper to me things
you've only ever shared with the moon
always a poetic tongue
whether it was in my mouth
or someone else's
your slow drawl spills secrets
into what little space is between us
you connect the stars of your past
and come alive before me like
a constellation in the night
we chase each swig of wine down
with a shotgun kiss
but I just know I'm intoxicated by
'The Way You Look Tonight'
Frank's serenading us, reminding me that
'I'm a Fool to Want You'
we only exist on borrowed time
and in stolen moments
but 'Lay Me Down' in the sand
spilling from our hourglass and
let me remember us this way forever

True colors

You begged me to fill your emptiness
color your canvas
paint you a masterpiece
I tried to wash over you like watercolor
but something about you was too stubborn
to let the pigment saturate
instead, you became the poetry
something I thought would be so beautiful
with my handwriting tattooed
over your scars
and my ink flowing
through your veins
but any rosy word I had in me
you scraped from the roof of my mouth
and swallowed to keep for yourself
hungry fingers dug deep into me and dragged out the
prose inscribed
deep into my bones
you devoured each and every letter
slurped down each syllable
that escaped from this silly lover's lips
and left me a plain white page
just like you used to be

I am an artist, but I cannot repaint your true colors

EVE

You reveled
in the sight of me
lying on your bed

your eyes caressed
my nude body
when you said,

You look like Eve

I wonder,
does that make you Adam?
or the serpent?

phoenix

HUNGRY LOVER

I do not want to / drag the "I love you" / from where it
must be / hidden deep down / in your throat / far from
where / you could say it to me / I do not want to / rip
your heart / from your chest / to hold it in my hands / to
try and find / the chamber meant for me / I am a hungry
lover / do not deprive me / of the essence I need

I WANT

I want to write a poem
that will hurt your feelings
I want the words to
pierce your armored heart
I want the shrapnel to be
so deeply lodged into your skin
you're pulling out the letters of my name
for the rest of your days
I want the poison of regret
to seep from your eyes
when your head hits the pillow at night
and I'm not nestled at your side

I want you to ache with the
violent desire for me

A POEM IN WHICH I ANALYZE HIS BIRTH CHART TO FIND
OUT WHAT WENT WRONG

It must've been your Virgo Sun
that made you strive for perfection / and we both know /
that we had our flaws / and we both know / that I never
could've been / good enough to be / your one and only /
you must've needed / to gather data / from multiple
experiments / test your hypothesis / on different women /
before getting your answer / and making your final
decision

Or was it your Cancer Moon
that made your "love" like water / I could only drown in
it / tsunami waves / wreaking havoc / on my once
harmonic earth / maybe your feelings / were too big for
you / to comprehend / too passionate / for you to make
sense of / or maybe / you felt nothing / at all /

Maybe it was your Virgo Venus
causing you to be so cautious / were you too afraid to be a
lover / or to be loved / critical overthinker / who tore me
apart / with your own anxieties / you never used your
heart / only half a brain / and you never let your soul /
guide you home

WONDERLAND

I've tumbled down this
rabbit hole thousands of times
and with each visit
to this wonderland
I feel the magic fade
the red melted right off of
the roses you gave me
and coated my hands
a bloody omen
you could no longer
conjure up the illusions I needed
and let the kingdom crumble
beneath us
it's nothing but black dust now
but sometimes I let myself in
through the looking glass
hoping to find you

CHURCH

You say you were never much
of a believer
but you kneel every Sunday
and pray for your sins
to be forgiven
so that you may be greeted
by the parting of golden gates
and taken into nirvana
you know your God
is a forgiving one
time and time again
She turns a blind eye
to your indiscretions
washes you clean
in Her river
and turns the water
to whiskey for you
She lights the fire that keeps you going
refusing to put it out even when
you turn and denounce Her,
curse Her name,
when you choose to believe in false prophets
She watches on as you fall from grace
and says a prayer for you, still

THE YEARS BETWEEN US

INSPIRED BY 'OUR STORY TOLD OUT OF ORDER' BY HEIDI WONG

1. you were the worst liar I had ever met / but something about your drunken southern drawl / and the way your eyes twinkled / under the Louisiana moon / made me believe / every word that / slipped off your silver tongue

2. I thought we spoke the same body language / you could say sorry / with a kiss / and the caress of your calloused hands / would leave me speechless / unable to argue with you / any longer / but that was all a lie / too

3. if you loved anything / it was being under the influence / of anyone or anything / that could get your sad heart pumping / you introduced me to the devil on my shoulder / the constant craving for a rush / for the incessant buzz of alcohol / or something a little more stimulating / you loved being high / more than you loved being mine

4. the sound of your seething voice / screaming / bloodshot eyes / and a pointed finger / as if I'm the one to blame / as if I shot the bullet / that killed our love / but it's my own blood on my hands

5. it was never a secret / that I wasn't your only / and I guess I didn't mind that / until I realized / I was finding solace / tucked under your chin / and hidden behind your arms / my face buried in your chest / I thought I heard your heart /

whispering my name / begging me to come closer

6. coffee and hot cocoa / I studied you / as you prepared it / like how an artist gazes / upon their muse / I knew in that moment I wanted to sketch every / inch of you / to keep you / forever

7. you used to accuse me / of sleeping around / as if you weren't doing it yourself / pointing the finger at me / as if I was the one to blame / for the shaky foundation / this castle was built upon / the king loved to get loud / and leave his fist in walls / demanding the truth / he had always been given

8. when it became unbearable / I remember crying / in your arms / late at night / in that dark / tiny room / you didn't wake / didn't even stir / maybe you snored a little louder / but I'm not truly sure / when I tried to push you away / you sleepily pulled me closer / and just like that / I was back under your spell

9. tangled up by the river / sipping on the smooth / we were called "lovebirds" / by passerby / and my heart swelled three sizes / you were lit aglow / by the setting sun / I had never seen / anything so beautiful / you told me / you wished you were an artist / like me / so you could capture that moment / in poetry / or a painting / and we collapsed into a kiss / as everything spun

10. the first time / you tried to kiss me / I wouldn't let you / instead I pretended to fall asleep /

resting my head on your arm / and closing my eyes / just wanting to soak in the moment / the feeling of being wanted / you kissed my hair / and my head / and hugged me close / and it was perfect / and sad all at once

11. I wonder if you loved me / or if you just loved to see me break / into a sacred mosaic / something of your own creation

12. I bet you think about me / while staring into your / glass of whiskey / gripping it so tensely / your knuckles go white / and you take a swig / but all you know now is / the bitter taste of loneliness / maybe you feel a pang of regret / or grief / or guilt / maybe it's just / the sting of liquor / slipping down your throat

13. I guess / you're not a monster / just a mere man / not a horned devil / but a human / whose demons / got the best of him / not a creature / who stalks women in the night / and steals their innocence / but a troubled boy / who knows nothing / but to feel pain / and inflict it

14. fourteen years between us / made me just the perfect age / to play your twisted games / you said we were just the same / something like twin flames / but you were the one who dug my grave / and disposed of my lifeless frame

ESCAPE

He tore his way into me
with tooth and nail
burrowed deeper
under my skin
like some kind of parasite
to use my body for his escape
my bones became his armor
he broke open the white gates
that locked up my chest
wove a robe from my muscles
and fed from my decaying heart
continuing on even as
I began to fester and rot
watched as sunshine yellow oozed
from wounds that withered me away
and left me

hopeless

ALL TOO WELL

Your whiskey-tinged memory still burns this sober throat / I tasted it on your lips / as you devoured me / you swallowed all of my sweet / and hated the sour / I became / memories of amber-hazed summer nights / dancing behind / tightly squeezed eyelids / back when we were / mania-fueled monsters / tearing each other apart / hot southern sun / melts us down / like the candles / I prayed to / and in the winter / we used my poems / as kindling / let it burn us down / to keep warm

SING FOR ME

I want to hear my name
spilling from your mouth
like a tsunami breaking over the shore
don't hold your tongue in my presence
sing for me until you run out of breath

UNHOLY

You took your rib
from its fortress
around your broken heart
and created me in your image
your unholy counterpart
don't you know that we were
never meant to stay here forever, lover?
a temptation too great
left two sinners bare in the light
now banned from the garden they grew
to wander hell on earth
alone

SNIP

I cut your name from its
embroidered home in
my mouth

it was the only way to
keep me from
calling for you

MERCY

I don't know how else to explain it / but it feels like
someone plunged both hands / into the middle of me /
and scooped out / all of the gooey / all of the soft and
smooth / left an empty carcass / and didn't even bother
for a funeral / I struggle with forgiveness / I don't want
to show mercy / why should I? / when it was not shown
to me?

IT'S ALMOST LIKE
YOU HURT ME
BECAUSE YOU
COULDN'T HAVE ME

KING MIDAS

Can't keep his hands to himself
he's been painting the town yellow
with his lecherous caress
bruising me a violent gold
and casting another with an aureate glow
he searches for a misplaced love
in the skins of the unsuspecting
trying girls on like jewelry
shining for no one to see
before they are long forgotten
like me
but now he's all alone
in his palace lit aglow with his greed
as much as he tries to fight it
this has always been his destiny

MOSAIC

All the kings' horses and all the kings' men
couldn't put me back together again
I've been gluing every broken fragment
of this shell into place
painstakingly, piece by piece
arranging myself into a new mosaic
and I hope that when the light hits

I blind you

STITCHING (REMINISCING)

I try to tiptoe around your vortex
careful not to overstep my self-imposed boundaries
long stretches of caution tape
wrapped over the holes of my heart
a weak attempt to deter my aching fingers
from digging inside
to pull out a black-and-white
memory of you
and use it to sop up the blood

But I get lost each time
sucked into the soft, romanticized folds
of "when it wasn't so bad"
where you could tuck me
behind your strong arms
and protect me from the guilt
when your lips on my neck
were enough to numb the ache

I'm angry at myself for growing far too big for that to be
enough anymore
I trade the bandage for a needle and thread

Burn

I exorcized you from me
doused myself in holy gasoline
struck a match against my bared teeth
and melted myself down
this time, it was my choice to
burn

HAPPIER

You used to call me on the telephone
so I could make you feel less alone
I listened to you murmur softly
drinking your words like cups of coffee
throughout the late night
not wanting to be the first to say goodbye
darling, when did it all change?
why did it all go away?
now I just lie awake
alone in bed, with only my heartache
I can't help but wonder
was I just the prey? and you, the hunter?
your love was like violence
bruised my heart a tender violet
you stole my innocence
and ruined me with your wickedness
if only you could see
how much happier I am
without you with me

Writer's block Part II

I don't think I have anything left to write about / and I know that can't be true / I've lived a life with sharp edges and shadows / so I can't understand why my tongue holds still / is that all my heart is willing to share? / just wilted love / and the slow rebuild / of an incredibly wrecked / heart? / have I finally stopped regurgitating the carefully constructed stories spit into my mouth? / shouldn't I rejoice in that? / healing? / why am I finding it somewhat unbearable to part with the pain? / isn't there more?

Loud

When I think of him
I think of how his vulnerabilities
tangled in this throat and how
he would rather choke on all of
those words I needed to hear
than sing along with me
I think of how he chose to stay
silent and how I need someone
who can be loud

THINGS I AM STILL FORGIVING MYSELF FOR
AFTER LACEY PAIGE RAMBURGER

Destroying myself so he would love me / destroying other people so I could love him / the entire time I was nineteen / the claws I've sharpened / the flesh I've torn / the blood I've spilled / the rotten words I've whispered / the axes I've ground / the poems I never write / the poems that / I do write / for ripping / hearts out of their chests and devouring them whole / for the web of lies I spun / for drinking in his false words like it was the voice of God / but never believing in myself

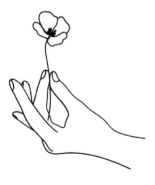

GROWTH

I look back at my growth
a steady rose rising from concrete
is it wrong to miss a past version of yourself
but still appreciate your new self?
I know I used to be softer, lighter
I know now that my arms are like daggers
and I'm too afraid to hold anything
too tightly
I know life is beautiful
but sometimes I am afraid to live it
I remember when I used to fight
for other people
like Athena with her arrows
always at war
but I fight for myself now

GENTLE

I wonder when I'll stop worrying if anyone loves me / I wonder when I'll know too much is too much / to tell myself that enough is enough / I've got to learn to stop watering plastic plants / just go to where the grass is greener / I've decided I'll try harder to not be mean / use this tongue to caress / instead of whip / I must learn to be gentle with myself / because the world will not be gentle with me

LITTLE DEATH

We wore the same-colored stripes
with the same stubborn faces
we cried for the same ghosts and
to the same gods
we were the stillness and
the roaring of the ocean waves
we were the same burn of
the summer skies

and it still did not prevent
us from dying our little death

fading away like a small star
into the morning light

"THE EARTH WILL TAKE CARE OF YOU"

A knife between my ribs
wasn't your only parting gift
you left me without shelter and without company
you spilled red wine on white carpet
but clearly, you don't mind ruining things

I spill salt into a circle and light my candles
I don't let it hurt anymore
I wear the scar like a shiny badge
I survived

you are forgiven but forbidden

UNSAID

You are the only person who needs to see your worth /
don't sell your soul / don't cut yourself up into pieces /
and throw them to the wolves / you should know you
deserve better than that / and better than what you have
now/ don't let anyone else tear you apart either / if it
must be done / you must do it / you must sew the pieces
back together yourself/ I wish you would understand this
/ if anyone comes for your heart you must protect it /
with everything in you / it's your most sacred thing /
remember that

Things I can't forgive you for

Stabbing me in my spine / with my own knife / spilling my blood / on hardwood floor / leaving me to clean up the mess / telling me / money is going to rent / telling me money is going to rent / while an eviction notice hangs on the door / now I'm homeless again / kicking me / when I was already / down on my knees / ruining that friendship / so perfectly / encouraging / my shadow self / to devour everything good / leaving me behind / I never thought you would

SAFE TRAVELS, OLD FRIEND

Two ships at sea
once led by the
same starlight
now drift apart
on two separate journeys
perhaps the wind
pushed one off path
unbeknownst to the other
until it was too late

FOR R. L.

I hope the angel who took your hand
wore the kindest face
I hope that you weren't afraid
I'm not sure where you are
but I hope it feels like an endless summer day
maybe something like your little place back in Maine
I hope that you're comfortable
and not feeling any pain
I hope that your Junebug is okay
and maybe one day
we'll share a laugh and an Irish coffee
like we used to

BITTER

I want to say that I'm not angry anymore / but the bitterness still coats my tongue / I swallow our mistakes / and wonder if you can still taste them too

ALONE

I don't know who I am
when I am alone
I am not sure I remember
how to be on my own
or how to fill the silence
without any noise

HAUNTING

Nothing has haunted the hallways of my mind
more ghoulishly than the ghosts of myself
versions that died peacefully, naturally
succumbing to divine timing
like snow melting under the spring sun
and others were ruthlessly self-sacrificed
or wrongfully gutted by others
but no one owes these shadows
a greater apology
than my surviving self
How could you? they wail,
How could you not have looked out for you?

GRIEF

Is the looming storm cloud
in the bright blue sky of my mind
it doesn't always rain
but when it does
it fucking pours

ANCHORS

Here I am carrying on
despite the false smile on my face
and my feet stuck like little anchors
in the rough waters of the past
I try to take a step forward
but find it too difficult to drag
my heavy heart with me
maybe one day the shackles will release me
something I won't mind leaving behind

A NOTE FROM NYC

I am the sun setting
on the city skyline
and I will rise again

VENUS

Born from blood and beauty
licked clean by the waves
of the Pontchartrain
I rise from the water like Venus
a sweet southern woman
with a taste for fire

THAW

Iridescent tears
run down the new
pink in her cheeks
the heat of them
part her lips as
they continue to pour
an exhale escapes
and her eyes
open wide
the warmth spreads
to her hands and
she wipes away her cries
she is now standing tall
finally thawed

so
she unfurls

and blooms

QUEEN

I hide away
in the tallest tower
I keep my hair cut short
and the windows closed
I do not yearn for the outside world
that is waiting patiently
beyond my iron gates
mouth open, teeth gleaming
I will not let myself be consumed by it

princes eager to rescue me
try desperately to slay
the dragon guarding my retreat
begging me to go
based on beauty alone
they know nothing of
this war-torn heart

I choose to revel in my lonely
I soak in the sticky sunlight
and sing with the birds
love songs composed
for my soul only

In the ashes of my ruined self
I find the strength to carry on

SHE IS A ROSE, JUST MIND HER THORNS

Have you ever heard that roses are one of the most difficult blooms to tend to? Yet they seem to be everyone's favorite flower. When you see them growing, do you stop to appreciate their beauty? Or do you try to yank it from the bush they grow from? To keep them for yourself? But you forgot that roses grow thorns along their stem. Protection. Armor.

You can look but don't touch / not unless you're willing to bleed for me

SOUL RECOGNITION

Have we met before?
you're looking into my eyes
I'm gazing into yours
do you think you had once been mine
In some other place or time?

A SEVEN-WORD STORY FOR A KISS

Two waves crash against
each other endlessly

STAY

An indigo night
a dark moon
looking down upon us
clouds from our mouths
drift up into crisp air
I hold your warm hands
kiss your palms
and ask you to
stay

and you do

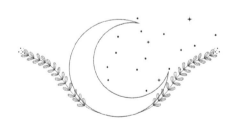

BEFORE YOU

I only knew love to be violent / a fiery crimson / that burned me down / to the bone / I only knew of / tense / raised fists / and tongues like a whip / lashing / I did not know / of gentleness / or even kindness / and you showed my wild self / those things / you tamed the soft animal / that is my heart / brought me from the brink / of death / and watched on as I took flight again

STORM CHASER

I felt frozen for all of my life
until I met someone
who struck a match
to all I ever knew
and melted me down
into a tidal wave
that soon devoured him
and all who stood in my path

but you were foolish enough
to sail into this Tempestas' heart
you were never frightened
even when my tears flooded us over
or when my wind whipped your face
reddened your cheeks and pushed you away

even when you could barely make it
through this violent rain
you never spiraled into a storm yourself
you called the clouds to part
and pulled the sunshine back through
sung to the birds and invited them back home
and welcomed me into your loving arms

phoenix

I YEARN TO WRITE YOU A LOVE POEM

But I'm busy catching each gentle word
that spills from your holy tongue
it becomes my scripture
I've prayed to false gods all my life
but this might be the real thing
how forgiving, how accepting
you are
even as I confess all of my darkest truths
your light never wavers

SOLACE

I daydream in pools
of emerald green
an effortless smile
on my tired mouth
I dip my toes into
the warm water
as I take one last look
at the stretches of
golden light peeking
through the trees
my eyes flutter to
a close and I breathe in

I know that I am safe here

TRUE RELIGION

My boy praises a
no-good goddess
he is baptized
swimming in my
"too big" brown eyes
he sings hymns
to the mid of
my thighs
I am his
he is mine

ILY

I guess I'll choke on
the truth in my throat
because I can't be brave
like I used to
my voice gets lost
in my throat anyway
or maybe I can say it
in other words and pretend that
those three don't exist
but in a language without
"I love you"
what do you say?

JAMES DEAN TO MY MARILYN

I'm breaking down again
you're begging me to let you in
and with your pretty eyes
you tell me I'll be fine
hold me as I burn
we watch the world turn
blue jean fantasy
it's just you and me
basking in a rose gold glow
don't let me go
you know I don't like to be alone
pretty baby
what's on your mind
can you give me a smile?
I'll stay here a while
I'll help you get by

THIS LOVE

This love is crimson / orange / and blue / radiating heat /
like the three o'clock sun / maybe I'm trying to say that /
we're the brightest star / in all of the skies / or that / I
only revolve / around you / all I know is / like the fabled
phoenix / this burning / brings my soul back home / your
floral touch / makes life grow / in all the / rotten parts of
me / and / I am eternally yours / even when / I take my
final breath / through death / and beyond

PIECES 2.0

You've loved me / to pieces / and back together again / healed the bruises / muddled across my skin / and mended the cracks / in my skeleton / with a mere / touch of your hand / you've loved me / back to light / back to life / discovered me in darkness / and refused to leave me there / you've calmed / the stormy sea / that is my heart / and brought breath back into my lungs / you've taught this heart to beat / rhythmically / again / and it'll be singing in tune / with you / for the rest of my days

HIGHLIGHT REEL

You're deep in sweet slumber
my heart is beating in time with your breathing
counting down the moments until you will wake and
I may suckle the honey from your soft mouth and
dance in the wildflower fields in your eyes
I'm wondering what saccharine scenes
are playing on your mind's film screen
I hope that I'm on the highlight reel

BREATHING

Loving you is as easy as breathing
what I mean by that is
I don't have to tell my body to do so
it happens naturally, almost magically
like each steady thump of my heart
like loving you is keeping me alive

YOU WILL BURY ME BEFORE I BURY YOU
AFTER HALSEY

If I should die before I wake,
I pray the Lord *my* soul to take
because if you were to be buried
before me
I wouldn't be able to breathe
even though this is a love that can transcend death
not everything can be safely kept
I know one day the time will come
when you must return to the place you came from
if I could, I would switch places with you
and show you that my love is true
a few years had to go by
for me to realize
what I've always known
that I'd rather spend eternity by your side
than be all alone

COFFEE

Holding me gently with two hands
your lips settle softly onto me
and you drink in the pure essence
of my energy
you love how I shock your senses
electrifying every inch of your skin
bringing life to the sleepiest parts of you
and I feel ever so lucky
to be the one to provide you with the
warmth you crave

To be surrounded by so
many beating hearts and still
be deafened by the sound of your own

LIMBO

Dancing on a tightrope
the line between my reality
and my insanity
terrified, I stay steady
curious, I look down
almost daring myself to
purposefully slip and
descend into madness

how tiring it is to teeter so
precariously in this limbo

THE BEAST

Depression swallows me whole
and keeps me safe and sound in its belly
this is not the first time it has happened
I know I must scratch my way through
rip through aching madness
to fall to the cold, hard ground
like some kind of twisted rebirth

I try not to move too abruptly
I try not to bother the monster
I lie quietly and try not to cry
it is I who has been clawed open

and I don't know
if I'll be able to escape this time

BIGGER

Sometimes it crashes over me
like a tidal wave
dragging me down to the
shadowy depths of my soul
where I remain trapped

I must face myself in the mirror
this is not an easy feat for someone like me
you don't know what terrifying
thing you might have to see

other times it's like being at a party
one I don't ever want to leave
a place with beautiful lights and colors
a rampage of people
and I'm in the center of it all
with the spotlight on me
the drinks are on me too

I'm in the upstairs bedroom
with a beautiful stranger
I'm the talk of the downstairs demons
I'm driving one hundred miles per hour

you'll never catch me
you'll never stop me
when I make it to the beach
I put my feet in the sand

I wade into the water
then it starts all over

but I am bigger than bipolar disorder
I will not let it chew me up and spit me out
I am stronger
I will get through this

phoenix

IN COLLABORATION WITH ALLYSON TYRA

When my eyes refuse to shut and my heart turns into a hummingbird / I know that I'm a god again / getting high off my own happiness / dancing to only the music in my mind / this is what it feels like to be invincible unstoppable / indestructible / to laugh in the face of death / and spit on the graves of those who have hurt you / this is a negative sign on your bank account / this is lust / and rage / and euphoria / this is not caring about anything other than the moment / and seeing the look in your lover's eyes/ when they tell you / that you're scaring them / when I become / a mess of / knotted hair / and unwashed clothes / reckless / breathless / and tear-stained / I know that / I am getting bad again / I am nothing but a ghost / haunting this bloody battleground / begging for another chance / to face my demons

TOXIC POSITIVITY

He says,
This is getting a little old,
don't you know?
I think the devil's got a hold
on your soul.
You should just pray
all of your sadness and worries away.
Don't let Lucifer lead you astray.
It'll be alright.
You're fine.
It's all in your mind.

I think,
How could you say that to me?
these are wounds you cannot see
but they are still bleeding.
I can find my own healing
without kneeling
to something that might not be.

GASOLINE

I am not this girl you've been creating
the real me feels like she is fading
I am not some kind of living daydream
or someone who stepped out of a magazine
I am not a plant whose leaves remain evergreen

I am not a monster but a beast
cackling as you fall to your knees
I've never been a dainty thing
don't you see?

Pure venom pumps
through my bloodstream
my kiss is like gasoline
I'll strike a match on my teeth
dance in your light as you
burn down before me

TW: SELF-HARM

CHERRY

The body reflected in the glass
does not mirror what's in my mind
the thoughts that I'm having are rather unkind

I imagine taking scissors to my skin
and cutting it all away
watch it all fall to my feet and decay

then maybe I will look how I'm supposed to
how everyone wants
with long legs, a flat tummy and a big butt

maybe I can take the soft in my belly
and force it elsewhere
maybe I will feel better if I cut my hair

I grab fistfuls of my skin and I ache and ache
I'm not sure how much more I can take

so I put on a dress with a cherry print
and smear rouge on my cracked lips
this is what I do when I feel like this

CHAMELEON GIRL

Changing her colors
shielding her third face
so you won't see the
pearl emptiness that weighs
heavy in her bones
or the stormy sea-colored insecurities
that saturate her entirely
she tries to hide the hurt by being
perfect in primrose
like the last light of the sun
forever setting in her eyes
she runs through color
ashamed of her true self
though her beauty
is obvious to everyone else
she is blind to it
this is the curse of the
chameleon girl

ACCEPTANCE

I'm dancing in the debris
of my shattered past
pieces of my previous lives
rain down around me
I twirl endlessly
my feet lifting
then stomping
into fragments of an
old fantasy
I raise my arms
above my head
and feel my wishes
slide through my fingers
and settle into my hair
the shell that once was
has been smashed open
the *truth* now pours down over me
still, I dance
tears roll from my eyes
and sweat trickles down my forehead
the brutal honesty of it all
envelops me in a spotlight
there is no hiding from it now

HEALING

I'm still pulling thorns from my skin
but it doesn't hurt as much as it used to

A LETTER TO MY YOUNGER SELF

When someone tells you that you are strong, believe them. You are willing to suffer for your happiness. It is up to you to decide if that's a flaw or skill. Your best moments will be spent under constellations, in the company of others. You will learn vulnerability. Intimacy. That you are capable of love. Again, you decide if that is a flaw or a skill. The older you get the more you will lose your mind. It's okay—you will learn how to find it again. You will reassemble it with new pieces. If you love something, let it go. That means your self, too.

TECHNICOLOR

I see the sun peeking at me from behind the horizon. A slow burn of brilliant orange cascading over the gray. I can even feel the gentle kiss of warmth on the tip of my nose. Yet the cold grip of my anxiety still has me trapped. Dissatisfaction discolors the edges of my scene. A new day is rising. I can see it right in front of me. I could almost reach out and grab a handful of the pure light. So why am I so stuck in the gray of today? Shrouded in the dark of the past, I yearn for the future where everything must be technicolor.

I MAY BE A ROMANTIC, BUT I AM *NOT* HOPELESS

BLOOMING

This body is growing softer every day
so I remind myself that

flowers are supposed to bloom with proper love and care

FERAL

I'm your wild woman
red-lipped and bared teeth
but you wouldn't dare keep me in a cage
you'd rather keep me around to touch
brush out these matted curls
and scrub the blood away
you don't mind my carelessness
even when I lick the bones clean
and throw them over my shoulder
or when I spend my nights
howling at the moon
with you burying whatever mess
I made that night
you make love to the monster
that lives under your bed
you'll lose me when the lights come on
but you don't mind
you fucking love the chase
and I can never be caught

PRINCESSES

I cannot tell you how long
I've waited for a precious prince
brave enough to rescue me
a fated one, destined for my heart
for true love's kiss to bless these lips
to break the curse
to slay the dragon
to make me queen of a new kingdom

It took me some time to realize that
you don't need to be rescued
you don't need a king to rule
I share my crown with you, sister
we will do this together
break our own spells
kiss our own wounds

We may be princesses
but we are *not* damsels in distress

BARE

I lay my body bare to unforgiving brightness
that exposes every crooked curve
every tiger stripe tattooed on my thighs
wild curls springing from my crown
chipped fingernails and scarred arms
the sun kisses every inch of me
feverishly making love to me
in front of everyone
causing my olive skin to glow golden
I lazily lie out and soak it all in

HONEY

I am warm honey
and you are dying for a taste

but this love doesn't come without a sting

I'M SORRY IT TOOK SO LONG

I've decided that I will
no longer compare
myself to her or her or her
my body is not a cage
but a home that withstood
the strongest hurricanes
I've learned to treat my body
like a garden instead of a graveyard
to trace these curves is a true privilege
for this body was blessed by Aphrodite herself

phoenix

THE RAGDOLL PART II

Is learning how to find herself
every day she cuts a stitch loose
letting go of someone who
was so much a part of her
and it hurts so deeply
but she no longer has to
drag the dead weight with her

phoenix

FOR THE ONES WHO BURN AND BURN

Remember that
you are your beacon of hope
you are your warmth
and you are your own

there will be times when
the ones around you fear
your intensity, your power
they will complain that your
flames lick at their heels
and that your light
is too blinding

you won't listen
and you'll grow and grow and grow
you'll find the ones who will
feed your fire, not dampen it

you'll be comfortable with
your own warm body
and content with soaking
alone
in your sunlight

SUFFOCATING

I'm suffocating under history and old hopes / but I can't cry anymore / I'm digging through the scorched fragments / of my past lives / yearning for any glimpse of the end / but I'm buried under more ash / than I had thought / surprised to see / that each claw through the heaviness / doesn't expose any light / it only encourages me / to rip my way through harder / choking / hardly able to see / anything but / **BLACK** / and feel the burn of the heat / as it fades / I will not stop / until I reach light again

WARRIOR

I am a girl with a peculiar rage
something like a scaly creature wrapped
around my shoulders, poised to strike
I am an imposter
a girl who wears a kind face
a gentle mouth
that still spits obscenities
soft hands that can still
hold a sword and shield
I think of myself as a warrior or hero
someone who needs no rescuing
I've fought for this kingdom
and I won't give it up to you
I run with wolves and
scream with the crows
I became one with the wild
you should be afraid

SPRING IS HERE AGAIN

Every year she presents a gift to me
wrapped in silk paper
all done up with a brilliant bow
always pushed into my hands
with an eager smile upon her face
like every year, she brings renewal
she brings me seeds
hoping that this time I will let them take root
she brings me a mirror and says,
Look how much you've grown!
she shows me how tenderness
has bloomed in my eyes
there's a softness to my body
that I would've never let grow before
she shows me my rose-colored heart and
all of the love held inside it

it is the greatest gift that I could receive

JOYFUL RISING

I love the crisp coolness of an early morning
the deep blue of the sky kissed blush
by the creeping sun
the stillness of everything
reflected in the soft dew coating
the grass, flowers, and leaves

I think it to be a magical time
smatterings of stars are still visible
though you wouldn't see them unless
you took a few moments to look up

the beginnings of a new day
ready to be unwrapped

LOVE

I am not who I love
I am not who has loved me
I am love in its entirety

INSECURITY

I'm sad to admit how long it took me to become familiar
with my own face
how long it took to tolerate more than a mere glance of
my reflection
some days I still find myself shielded from the light, for
fear of being seen
but this skin is like a landscape
with mountains and valleys
splashes of sunset on stretches of olive complexion
I've learned to not be ashamed
of my war with myself
of fighting the uphill battle of self-love
I'm just a battered soul
reciting affirmations
in the mirror
too

PHOENIX

I didn't rise from the ashes
I tore through them
clawed under the black heaviness
until my nails were broken and bloody
and my throat was raw
after being blind to the light for so long
I didn't understand
why I had to burn

until I finally took flight

KINTSUGI

I am washed in great gilded light
forgiving warmth spilling all over me
casting me in a vintage glow
the rays wrap me in such a tender embrace
I forget all of my heartbreak
and the cracks in my shell have been filled
with holy gold

SOMEWHERE NEW

Take me out of this room
and bring me someplace new
show me all Gaia has created
all for which She is celebrated
let's go to the bayou
up to the mountains too
show me oceans crystal clear
and I'll smile from ear to ear
show me warm desert sand
acres of deep green land
I want to go to the big city
where the lights are bright and pretty
I don't want to be home
where I am all alone
I want to watch the world
collapse and unfurl

phoenix

FOR SARAH

A girl like a gun
an Aries sun
you keep burning on
for everyone
a rolling stone queen
at the age of nineteen
photographed taking roses from Greta Van Fleet
you stand at about five two
and you don't let nobody tell you
nothing
still standing strong
after all the suffering

you inspire me more than you'll ever know

WHO ARE YOU?

A melancholic madonna,
perfectionist prima donna,
tempest temptation,
haunting hallucination

FULL MOON IN SCORPIO

Bathing under the light
of the pink moon
scrubbing myself clean
of all the sticky residue
so that my inner light
can shine through
shedding the skin
of a younger me
writing eulogies
for all my fatalities
splitting at my seams
trying to find some kind of meaning
discovering who I am supposed to be
finally seeing all of the possibilities

I ACHE FOR THE WOMAN I COULD'VE BEEN

If all the pieces of my life
had fallen into the right places
I celebrate her innocence and her naivete
while I mourn mine
I wonder who she would be
the me who didn't endure tragedy
would she still be strong and resilient?
compassionate or kind?
if gray had never crept into the colors of my life
would I still be the same?
if I had never known a sky with rain
would I still be who I am today?

ADVENTURE

The anonymity of a big city / is ever so tempting / I remember how / I grew in the cracks / of New York sidewalk / springing upwards / like a stubborn weed / just starting to take the shape / of the woman I will be / I think back to Nashville / and how I finally found my voice / whistling through the wind / a loose melody / soon developing into a symphony / is it wrong to say / that I just want to escape? / all I know is / every time I step foot / outside of my door / I find myself a little more / putting the pieces of my puzzle together / with each new adventure

VISITING MY HOMETOWN, 13 YEARS LATER

I feel like a child again
walking through a phantom city
that has grown bigger than me
streets that stretch like muscle
I call it the heart of California
and it beats only for me
I am its flesh and blood
I suckled on the lavender air and cigarette smoke
bloodied my knees on the concrete
and lost my milk teeth
here
in this place that no longer remembers me
I am a foreigner in a mysterious land
with the traces of Louisiana tangled in my hair
and thick honey dripping from my voice
when I speak
surprising the family that hasn't seen me in years
I am both the bayou and the Bay Area
a small-town city girl
just trying to find her place in the world

phoenix

FROM NOW ON

I will grow flowers
in my hair
instead of my lungs
I will not allow myself
to be silenced
I will not hide
what makes me
beautiful

HIDING

Like la lune
our evening queen
I kept parts of myself dark
rarely allowing my
entirety to be exposed
in my youth, I covered
my face with a cascade of curls
an anxious expression
masked by a book
as I grow older
I have become less keen on
hiding my shine
I let it go
and let me glow

phoenix

I AM ONLY WHO I AM RIGHT NOW

Extending an olive branch
to my shattered mirror
an apology for all the ways
I've ruined myself
a ragdoll stands before me
tattered stitches and scraps
hardly in one piece
but still firmly on two feet
shreds of my past mistakes
flutter to the ground
a weight slowly disappears from my shoulders
I am illuminated in the light of forgiveness
lit aglow with self-love

THE LOVE SONG OF A MADWOMAN

Is sung through gap teeth
and red lipstick
it echoes throughout the
caverns of your infinite mind
a haunting siren's call
luring you to the edge of insanity
will you jump?
plummet into the world of the wild?
let your soul escape
and roam the bountiful earth?
or will you stay comfortably
inside your itchy skin?
a voice like broken glass
scratching deep into your ears
an inescapable melody
wailing endlessly
will you answer her call?

I AM THE GOD OF REBIRTH

Do you know / what it's like to die? / to be torn down /
into nothing / by your own hands? / to burn / in the fires /
that you've set yourself? / there is a god of death / but
they never tell you / about me / and how I rise / from the
ashes / every time / I am knocked down / I am the god /
of what comes after / the ache is gone / I am what /
makes flowers grow / in the wounded parts of you / I
bring forth the light / to flush out the darkness / I will
show you / how to claw your way / out of the ash / and fly
again

deveree extein

MY BODY IS MY GREATEST WORK OF ART

I was sculpted by wise hands
from the top of my head
to the curve of my swollen belly
down to my size ten feet
every feature was shaped purposefully
to frame the gap in my teeth
the frizzy curl of my hair
or the acne sprinkled across my face
each brushstroke was carefully placed
so that all my flaws could make up
this masterpiece

deveree extein

phoenix

INDEX

NOTES

"Ophelia" references a character from William Shakespeare's drama Hamlet

"Paper girl" was originally published by Honeyfire Literary Magazine

"When (otherwise) peaceful women go berserk, what ticks them off" title references a Cosmopolitan magazine article title from September 1990

"Things I am still forgiving myself for" was inspired by a poem by the same title by Lacey Paige Ramburger

"The years between us" was inspired by "Our Story Told Out of Order" by Heidi Wong

"Queen" was originally published by Red Planet Magazine

"You will bury me before I bury you" references lyrics from "Ya'aburnee" by Halsey and "Now I lay me down to sleep" published by The New England Primer

"Chameleon Girl" and "Healing" were originally published by Other Worldly Women Press

"Warrior" was originally published by Sledgehammer Lit

"Spring is here again" was originally published by
Auroras and Blossoms NaPoWriMo Anthology 2020

RESOURCES

There's nothing wrong with needing a little help sometimes. Please reach out to any of the following if you feel like you need to.

Suicide and Crisis Lifeline - 988

Crisis Text Line - Text HOME to 741741

National Sexual Assault Hotline - 1-800-656-4673

ABOUT THE AUTHOR

Deveree Extein lives deep in the Louisiana swamp with her kitten, Luna. When she isn't writing, she likes to paint, play guitar (badly), and watch *Gone with the Wind*. She is also the author of a chapbook, Flicker: poems. Find her online @bydeveree